DEBRIS

DEBRIS

DANIEL HUWS

CARCANET POETRY

First published in Great Britain in 2025 by
Carcanet
Main Library, The University of Manchester
Oxford Road, Manchester, M13 9PP
www.carcanet.co.uk

Text copyright © Daniel Huws 2025

The right of Daniel Huws be identified as the author
of this work has been asserted in accordance with the
Copyright, Design and Patents Act of 1988; all rights reserved.
No part of this book may be used or reproduced in any manner
for the purpose of training artificial intelligence technologies or systems.

A CIP catalogue record for this book is
available from the British Library.

ISBN 978 1 80017 522 8

Book design by Andrew Latimer, Carcanet
Typesetting by LiteBook Prepress Services
Printed in Great Britain by SRP Ltd, Exeter, Devon

The publisher acknowledges financial
assistance from Arts Council England.

CONTENTS

Author's preface ... 9

I - NOTH

The Party	15
The Survivors	16
Escape	17
Waking in the Small Hours	18
Goodbye to Tudor	19
The Guard	20
The House	21
Three Riddles	22
Father O'Conscience	23
Even So	24
Nothing	25
A Mountain Land	26
The Ark	27
Sons of Men	28
The House of Self-destruction	29
Revenant	30
The Knot	31
O Mountain	32
The Voice of a Child	33
Give Me a Medal	34
The Oranges Won't Grow	35
The Burden	36
Amends	37
Is the Snow Your Whole Love?	38
For Better for Worse	39
Like a Stone	40
Who Can We Blame	41
Wedlock's Summer	42
The Call of the Ring	43

The Office	44
Rendez-vous	45
Four Appropriations	46
Sitting Tenant	47
In the Café	48
Feelers	49
Three Nursery Rhymes	50
Crime Passionnel	51
A Voice	52
A Dawn	53
On the Mountain	54
Playing With Fire	55
Alpines	56
Message	57
Eyes	58
The Villetta	59
The Piercing Wind	60

II – POEMS FIRST COLLECTED IN *THE QUARRY*

From an Old Songbook	63
The Guardians	64
The Priest's Confession	65
The Print	66
Goodbye	67
The Quarry	68
New Moon	69
Indelicate	70
Three Its	71
Palais d'Amour	72
As When	73
A Cadence	74
The Slow Way	75
More than Glass	76

Peace	77
Silence	78
First Night	79
Hillfort	80
The Ornithologist's Friend	81
At the Root of Being	82
Mercy	83
The Edge of a Playground	84
The Rock	85
A Winter Calendar	86
Woodsmoke	88
Al Poco Giorno	89

III – UNCOLLECTED POEMS

Goldberg Variations	93
When the Lark Sang	94
Blocks	95
The Long Garden	96
The Old Man and His Mare	97
Old Psychic	98
Fraying Clouds	99
Catatonic Schizophrenia 1995	100
HMS *Thetis*	101
A Kite's Flight	102
The Lifeline	103
Honey	104
In North Japan	105
Three Sisters	106
Dew	107
The Burial	108
Eight Years On	109
Lay-by	110
Salt	111

Comfort	112
Lost Cove	113
A Heart	114
Debris	115
The Truth	116
Gorse	117
A Survivor	118
The Hob	119
The Pebble	120
Umbrellas	121
The Bed	122

IV — OCCASIONAL POEMS

Birthday Poem for Jean Hawkes	125
To Ted Hughes on his Appointment as Poet Laureate	126
Letter to Ted and Luke	128

AUTHOR'S PREFACE

Readers know an editor can make an author. In 1999 I came to know Christopher Reid. For Faber, he edited my volume of poems, *The Quarry*. He was a marvellous editor; even the title chosen was his. In 2024, a chance meeting brought us together again. *Debris* has its roots in that meeting. The idea of a 'Collected Poems' was Christopher's, and in making the selection that became 'Collected', I generally followed his guidance. Thanks to him, a number of early poems, excluded from Noth, now find their way into print, while a few 'occasional poems' that had found their way into print now slip away, dismissed. The volume is further indebted to Christpher for his patience and for his uncanny eye and ear, ever alert to the cumbersome word or phrase, or to a jarring note.

The poems assembled here span a period of seventy years, a period that embraced long silences, one lasting from 1972 until 1986, when professional duties and family life filled my days. At no time during those seven decades were poems more than personal therapy, or light diversion. They were never a vocation.

Many thanks are due to my daughter Hanna for her diligence in transmuting the poems in this book into digital form. Finally my thanks are due to John McAuliffe at Carcanet Press for undertaking this publication.

To Helga

I

NOTH

THE PARTY

'All I meet is Tom, Dick and Harry
Where I hoped for a girl who would change it all.
To make this a party not a funeral
A good deal of drink seems necessary.'

So he drank and his drollery made them all laugh
Till they cried. They thought him the wonder of men.
But the crowd did not grow on his fancy and when
The room began swimming he thought he'd be off.

They pleaded with him, they gently urged
'The party's not yet over, come,
Just one more drink.' But right away home
On twelve staggering legs he lurched.

The front door slammed like a thunder of stones.
So sound they slept, not a neighbour stirred.
The air was close and he was tired.
He took off his flesh and lay in his bones.

THE SURVIVORS

Survival would be the pick of a poor bunch:
Such was our joke, after a week adrift,
Tormented by the weather and racked at night
On the couches of phantasmal mermaids.

Yet a sun-fed paradise the island
In whose embrace we re-awoke to life
Promised our husbandry, we thought,
Once we had laid our apprehension.

But the natives whose hostility we feared
Kept to the forest like wild creatures.
Nature turned so lavish in her bounty
That labour would have seemed ingratitude.

If you love you could call such blest habitation
It turned suicide by love-in-idleness,
Which pretty flower was nature's abundance,
And the days of dying bred spite in our tongues.

Their dissension whetted a blade of violence
Which one by one picked off our company
Till of a stalwart dozen alone remained
Besides myself John Pity and Jack Pride.

Soon Jack confided: her bounty is yet a knife
Thrust at our hearts. And we two, rashly wise,
In a night of unpremeditated action
Repaired the boat and stole to sea again.

ESCAPE

To have woken into the clear of evening
With the tired feet wandering as they please
Across the avenues of an orchard
Where green cherries are thick on the trees,

And beyond the lane where the barbarous scent
Of mayflower billowed as did its white foam
In the short hour that is not yet night
To have strayed in a wood which seemed like home,

Where birch was birch and oak true oak
And their leaves spread a darkening green.
So much was certain. But the ringing song
Was of birds more nameless than they ever have been.

WAKING IN THE SMALL HOURS

Suppose you had slept in a room for half a year
And never known that the little patch of sky
Visible from your bed, no larger than a pane,
Lay in the path of the moon.

You awake in the small hours and a foot away
On the colourless pillow two pinhead-sized full moons
Are reflected in the grey eyes staring past you
From a luminous white face.

Can wives be allowed such night-time liberties?
To startle honest husbands out of their wits,
To wander centuries away, to bind themselves
To the moon, with the gaze of a corpse?

GOODBYE TO TUDOR

In forgiving mood, this sultry July afternoon,
The last lingering child will be gone
From the gates of Tudor Secondary Modern School,
A school most teachers gratefully shun.

The intimate daily struggle so calmly ends,
Without victory to either side.
Goodbye to the staff and to the boys more sadly
And the girls most sadly I have replied.

And a friend offers congratulations, echoing
Complaints I should have kept unsaid:
'My God, you must be glad to leave.' My children,
For his ignorance I could strike him dead.

THE GUARD

I'd hardly closed my eyes, I can't have been dreaming,
When suddenly the room in which I lay
I knew was a prison; escape, my single thought.

The door fell open sweetly, the passage held
Nothing to daunt me but silence and near-darkness
(Could freedom be so easy?), on I hurried
Down flights of stone steps into a maze
Of narrow vaulted corridors where sunlight
Shone from distant ends. This way, then that,
As often as I neared the light I stopped
And from each arched doorway drew back.
He stood there every time.
The same monitory figure in uniform,
His unsmiling face, though aged and vacant and grey,
None but my very own, barring the way.

THE HOUSE

Three hundred and sixty-five rooms?
And fifty-two stairways?
And all of us here guests?
And then, our host?

Here now is far from the music,
I wander further.
There was this haunting gaze
Of recognition.

Hope and a bump of the heart
Open each door.
Always, transfixed in gesture,
Doll-like strangers.

And tongueless am I to answer
Their dumb surprise,
Nor can a look convey
She is not here.

And those eyes may be only a dream
That is slow to fade.
And I might have been drinking and dancing
Or packing for home.

THREE RIDDLES

I first beheld her in the morning light
(I had come by night), naked where I undressed her,
And through her body a new world she revealed
To me, a stranger. Nothing her heart concealed.

But when I visited her in the moonless night
By candlelight she was inscrutable,
And mocked, favouring me with nothing but
A delineation of the idiot figure I cut.

        ***

A young man older than the hills
Made me his bride.
The first of my many children were old
When I was born.
Some I suckled at my breast
You call my fathers.

        ***

Horn the devil may be
Yet he is hornless.
Bone the devil may be
Yet he is boneless.
My flesh and blood he is indeed
But he is no child of mine.

FATHER O'CONSCIENCE

Father O'Conscience whispered to me
'Listen, my son, the life that's best
For the likes of yourself is the one you've found.
Don't be codded by memory
Into thinking you were happy shambling around
With a parcel of mortals on your chest.'

EVEN SO

You were so beautiful, he so unwise
To protract an exchange that led to nothing.
If you'd studied his hands instead of his eyes
You might have guessed why, and even so
He'd have earned your shrug when you got up to go.

NOTHING

You appear again, more beautiful than ever,
And still he makes no move. Is he unmanned?
Nothing can spell the terrible word never
When it's made of gold. Look at his left hand.

A MOUNTAIN LAND

Broad-plained neighbours suspiciously circle
Our land of mountain; to whose small eyes
Our smiling self-sufficiency
Must speak riches.
One then another,
Time and again they mass their borders,
Prepared for resistance we never offer.
The sortie here, the thrust there,
Whole armies trampling our countryside,
We give like air, take to the hills.
They never stay.
Nothing to plunder,
No one to conquer, their mettle rusts.
They leave, arrogant and disdainful
Of the empty land that rigged their hope.
And glad always to see their backs,
To know our immunity proved again,
We laugh at their crudeness and bafflement.

But our malcontents have a fine scorn
And a harsh name for the ancient wisdom
That keeps us free. They resent that fools
Should think us beggars, feel shame we never
Have shown the nerve to commit our lives
To the flat valleys, let a nation root
And bloom a flower of civilisation,
The being our richer selves a trophy
Continually to be battled for
In bloodshed in the mouths of valleys.

THE ARK

Since the last peak sank from sight
Nothing has broken the round horizon.

The water we floated on was fresh
The first weeks, now it is brackish.

My eyes swim with watching, swarm
With specks of white. But here, growing,
In a single speck in the lowering sky,
Homing, homing, my hope, my dove,
Back for a third time
With nothing.
                No olive branch
From the drowned earth, the drowned earth-life.
The world's womb has closed to the seed
Of vitality boxed in our dark hold.
My birds, my beasts, you mistook for a birthright
Your manless jungles, your days of freedom,
The providential counterpoise
To this afterlife on the face of the deep.

Below, the fetid animal aura,
The shuffling, stamping, the howls, the screeching,
May custom's deathly anaesthetic
Stifle the protest. We want no bedlam.
And may it be no impertinence
In the eyes of God to let out a dove
For occasional news of how things are looking,
The air and water, the water and air.

SONS OF MEN

Past dawn, past cockcrow, into the bright of day
They slumber on, hustled by morning's clamour
Never so far as to outrange the choice
Of the blissful slither back to annihilation.
Sleep, motherly sleep, clasp your sons
Till their eyelids spring open in surfeit; then as they scatter –
Defeated men, your matrix dark in their minds –
The rest of their ruined day you need fear no rival.

THE HOUSE OF SELF-DESTRUCTION

Ominously did the planets forgather
In the twelfth house so full of danger
To the crab in his massive shell who would rather
Sidle a mile than meet a stranger.

REVENANT

A boatman used to ferry me back down the river
To the watergate. Twelve slippery stone steps
And I'd fifty yards to go along the cobbles
Past skinny kids like maggots in the dust
And beggars asleep in the shade. Then, how cool
To enter the marbled hall, how composing
To climb the grand stair, how rich with silence
My noble rooms. Not a soul dared cross my sight.

The water laps the same massive foundations.
The groundfloor windows are grated still. But above
Are windows flung wide open and washing hung out.
Shrill tongues and a woman's raucous singing.
Proliferous humankind has come to stay.

Between the walls defaced, up the littered stairs,
I fight a way in the ebb and flow of children.
I am unknown. My friends are a dead species.
My servants are swallowed up in their own lives.
My beautiful courtesans will be prinking themselves
For boys on scooters.
What might marriage have saved?

I climb to the nuresmaid's garret. The door's ajar,
The room empty. Here it is almost quiet.
The sunshine is creeping inward over the tiles.
I tiptoe across to the open casement and shiver
In the sudden warmth. There are fishermen out on a raft.
The child again, I cringe from the sheer drop
To where the diminutive ripples coruscate.

THE KNOT

There is whispering in the nooks of the court.
Mr Secretary is at your ear.
You have your friends.
While you finger the umbilical cord
That reaches to Rome,
While you fumble with your knot
Of rights and wrongs,
Are there no swords in your kingdom?

How beautifully England lies
At your feet this morning of spring.
Shall the body have two masters?
What kind of head is it that is not supreme?
Shall a nation dwindle, O Harry,
Harry my king,
Because you cannot stop the ears of your mind
To an old woman's foreboding
That an innocent head or two will fall from the block?

O MOUNTAIN

We know our crags, our climbs, our controlled terrors,
As we know our own hearthsides. We manage nicely.

The clouds of selfishness rift and terribly
Turning our foothills small and grubby appears
The mountain soaring against a blue heaven,
Bulking beyond conceivable ascent.
Yet while we slept was a breaking body climbing.

Where the winds of the world pour unendingly
Wildly whistling to no one, let the mind hover
And its eye make out in the dazzle, O Mountain, O Man,
The frail figure on the white virgin peak.

THE VOICE OF A CHILD

With the eye of a flower, the eye of a child,
You looked at the world and saw the sun.
It was warm, it was kind, you grew towards it
Adoringly. Oh, it was marvellous.
Shade was the unmentionable.
That the universe could be so perfidious,
That the sun could blot right out, never
Could it happen. But happen it did
And the sun blotted right out and darkness
Swooped. And leaves and roots were as nothing.
With the voice of a flower, the voice of a child,
You cried against the iniquity
Of blackness, blackness clammy and choking
Whose rustlings circled like assassins,
Blackness that seemed to have no ending.
Your only resource was to flourish death
In a brilliant flare of uncomprehending.

GIVE ME A MEDAL

The voice that had breathed down their necks,
On whose strings they had danced,
Floated away beyond the trees,
Left them presenting arms on the parched square,
An infinite blankness the point of their stare.

A mate is gibbering, a mate is our cold,
Will our hero not break ranks, stir to their aid?
He doesn't bat an eye. God, give him a medal,
Your most beautiful fucking soldier on parade.

THE ORANGES WON'T GROW

The oranges won't grow,
The oranges won't grow,
Do you think I'm surprised?
Do you think I don't know?
I heard you say so
Several years ago,
More than once, more than twice.
Could have told you as much,
Could have told you myself,
Even longer ago,
When we stood there in Paris
To say cheerio
And you clutched your ticket,
Your airline ticket
For Greenland.

THE BURDEN

A rush of disregard, a protruding stone,
A moment of sick-faint at the crack of glass:
No other demijohn in the world can help you,
Watching the wine pulsing into the ground.

AMENDS

The play tight, the scrums countless,
Bored and shivering out on the wing,
What sort of game are you in?

The field suddenly opens wide.
The joy of lengthening your stride.

IS THE SNOW YOUR WHOLE LOVE?

For long hours the toys have lain neglected.
A face settles to glumness at the window.
Onto the paths and grass, onto the hedges,
Onto the fields and wood the flakes feather,
Down, down, to instant evanescence.
Must it be a winter without snow?

Child, child, is the snow your whole love?
Is a winter your whole lifetime?
The sky may exhaust itself in vain. Learn
To accommodate your adversary, the earth.
Snow is accidental to her gestations.
Her moods are yours for the taking, but not to be mended.

FOR BETTER FOR WORSE

The children are all asleep.
They have filled my day
As in a few years
Their absence will.
The bomeland in which no longer
Should I feel at home
Is beyond the sea.
A room away my husband broods
On himself only
If he hasn't gone to bed.

There is all this heap of mending.

I am so lonely.

LIKE A STONE

When not asleep I could hear the air's faint humming,
The unmown grass was cool to the limbs, the sun
Was a glow beyond the walls of the eye's red womb.

I hear your approach, a light swishing of grass.
Blue-grey was the glaring world to my open eyes,
And there was your outstretched arm, unwavering, pale,
Holding the russet fruit
So sternly towards me, with not a word, and your eyes
As I'd never seen them before. My will was yours.

In gratuitousness your action wanted nothing.
Can a man not be left to drowse in the sun on his own?
That was a place where I could have lain for ever,
Like a cat, like a lizard, like a stone.

WHO CAN WE BLAME

The hours of beauty sleep,
The concentration at the looking-glass,
The struggling into a dress.

The studied entrances,
The rooms of peering faces,
And nobody there at all
You could ever want to impress.

O girls, who can we blame
But God, for inventing mirrors.

WEDLOCK'S SUMMER

A billion blades of grass,
A hundred sodden roses,
Four swallows finding their wings,
Two asses rubbing noses.

THE CALL OF THE RING

He wasn't Napoleon or Byron or God.
He disapproved of trying to seem odd.
He'd cashed his life to skip and spar
And tonight he'd be greater than Tommy Farr.

There is no one to tell him it isn't his guts,
His feints, his footwork and uppercuts
That amaze the crowd that has stopped to stare
At a naked man fighting the air.

THE OFFICE

He was always the quiet sort,
Can't say I've really known him
Though I've been here as long as he has,
Thirty-three odd years.
Given his cushy old job,
A nice little wife, as they say, and decent kids, Christ
Knows what bug can have bitten him.

Well there he was at his desk,
Arms sort of pinioned to his chair
And body sort of thrust forward,
Staring out of the window
With this god-awful look on his face,

And as if we simply weren't there
In his deadly monotone
The poor old bugger was going on
About somebody called Elias.

RENDEZ-VOUS

Perhaps best not tomorrow
But thirty years tomorrow,
And find how the essences mingle
After time's distillation.

Thirty expectant years,
What a vigil for us to savour.
And how poignant will be our condolence
For the flight of what might have been.

How decidedly more adult,
How far more imaginative
Than to meet precariously now
Alive to what could be.

FOUR APPROPRIATIONS

Slow major rode ahead,
Slow captain stumbled after
To tell him all the squaddies were dead
Of an unidentified laughter.

***

His milk was untouched, the police were told,
His soup was congealed and his corpse was cold
And under his shirt they found a locket
Containing nothing and made of gold,
Containing nothing, not even, not even,
Not even a woman's hair.

***

He was ambling up through the field and moved in
For his run on the rails when what do you know
He got caught in a pocket till past the post
With a handful of horse and nowhere to go.

***

A length of linen of deadest white
Waiting for the morning light
And an old woman of failing sight
And thick of nail to sew me tight.

SITTING TENANT

So there was this Wisdom chappie on the ground floor,
Ever so poor and respectable, ever so courteous.
Even had you been able he wasn't the sort
You'd have the heart to eject.

Then you can't just watch an old guy slowly decay
On bread and butter. We started feeding him meals
And came in time to feed him our daily lives
With his buckshee sermons as pay.

And when we go out at night there he sits
Upholstering this coffin.
Not, he likes to observe, with his singular smile,
That he means to use it himself.

IN THE CAFÉ

Yes, he kept saying,
Ours was a beautiful revolution,
But we should have seen his.
Her eyes, he said,
I can't tell you.
He pulled out this old photograph.

> A photograph of a wide square
> Dotted with the small figures
> Of unmistakably grown-up men
> Caught in apparently private performance
> Of the several acts of stumbling
> And running and lying prone.

A sort of memento he explained,
The only one.
She would never give me her portrait.
Yes, it was certainly love,
Calf-love maybe,
All I have known.

> His mind was going.

FEELERS

The war goes dead.
The dead go uncounted.
New missiles are trained.
The General Staff
Is immured in conclave,
Teeth and tongue
Hatching new horror
In a blacked-out mouth.

They will not have been told
Of the peace feelers
Already out,
The hands and fingers
About their business
As they know how,
Gauche as Christ,
Adroit as the devil.

THREE NURSERY RHYMES

It rains and rains and rains and rains
More than anyone knows.
The butt is leaky, the butt is big,
It rarely overflows.

***

We found the table bare
And bare the larder shelves.
We slipped to an upper room
And helped ourselves to ourselves.

***

He should have known.
She should have known.
Let the driver say if it does him good he thought
Children did not run across the street at midnight.

CRIME PASSIONNEL

Curtain up, says the night sky.
Enter, two blokes.
Off, a bird's disconsolate noises.

And here they come once more, says the street,
Do they think I lead nowhere?
Am I a closed circuit?

The telephone cased in its kiosk
Hums and sighs.

The letter-box gapes.

No, I can't bear it,
Says the house-door, getting hysterical.
They're here again,
And this time they're coming indoors.
One of them's a maniac, can't you see,
And lethally armed.

Exactly says the night sky,
And as for that female party
Waiting for lover-boy,
If she can't cry herself to sleep
She's got a long night coming.

But the single-bed is a bed of the world
And croaks:
I won't say I care for corpses
No more than I care for murderers
But the two of you need some kip.
I'm easy.
Make yourselves welcome.

A VOICE

Mindlessly,
Year after year,
In the same month,
In the same spot,
In the same colours,
The orchids flower,
The orchids wither.

This is the wilderness
Where a voice is crying
For the helmeted men to roll up
With their yellow plant.

A DAWN

There was no sunrise,
Only a brightening,
And the mist
Moving among the stones
Grew visible.
And there was silence,
A silence growing
Around the unanswered voices
Adrift in the chasm below,

The lament of the sheep,
The call of crow,
The shuffle of shale down the scree.

ON THE MOUNTAIN

Flowers, flowers, flowers,
The mountain is moidering.

From beyond what ages of ice
Might a memory have carried?

Where have they known flowers,
These acres of rock and peat
Their cryptogams inhabit?

PLAYING WITH FIRE

Did your bonfire stream
To heaven in sparks
Or smoulder and sweat
And never flare?

I no more know
Than you can smell
The smoke in your hair.

ALPINES

The village in love
With the avalanche
Preens itself in the sun.

The lake in love
With the meteor
Licks its lips.

The glacier in love
With the next valley
Inches towards the sea.

MESSAGE

Message received
With difficulty
Voice seemed normal
Sends love
To couldn't catch who
No more position
Bound to conclude
Good way out
Batteries fading.

EYES

These wide-awake eyes
And starry skies
And eyes and eyes
And wrinkles and lashes
And cheeks and lips
And hands and hands
And thighs and thighs.

And there is this lidless eye
Raking the earth
And raking the sky
For darkness.

THE VILLETTA

Here is your villetta
With its view over the sea
Owned by the crooked lawyer.

Here is the shack
Of the fisherman
Ready to hire out his daughter.
Here is the office
Of the head of police
Who can fix a permit of sojourn

And might not be blind
To a gift
If the gift is made
In mortification,
The coin of the realm.

THE PIERCING WIND

Was there not wood to hew
And stone to quarry?
Had you not eyes?
Had you not hands?

The piercing wind questions.

Answerless,
I huddle behind children.

II

POEMS FIRST COLLECTED IN *THE QUARRY*

FROM AN OLD SONGBOOK

The girl was sensational, he was a creep,
His eyes were like pebbles while hers were so deep
That at night the thought of them left me no sleep
They so plainly knew something was lacking.

As I leaned on this tree I could only advise
That touch it or eat it sure nobody dies
Of a bite of the fruit that will open your eyes
Til like gods you gaze out on the garden.

But somehow we managed to cock up the show
By upsetting the gaffer, old who-do-you-know,
Your one with the voice who's accustomed to go
For his walk in the cool of the evening.

And she whom I love goes eating her bread
In the sweat of a bloke who'd be happier dead
While the horny heels come bruising my head
As I choke on the dust of the desert.

So you beasts of the field take warning by me
However so subtle you think you may be
Keep your tongues to yourselves or the Old Man will see
That you drag out your days on your bellies.

THE GUARDIANS

Lift your eyes to heaven
And you suddenly see them,
Two guardian angels,
High above the valley,
Moving apart,
Moving together,
Looping on invisible swell.

It isn't a love dance,
It isn't a duel,
They are feeding their young.

They nest high
In the tall oak
In the shrunken core
Of the old wood.

There is no other pair for miles.

THE PRIEST'S CONFESSION

Father, I'm troubled by Satan, afraid I begin
To discover his works in places where
My theology hadn't conceived them,
In coloured cloth and in agitation of air.

The enormity dawned when I met the widow's daughter
(a woman by now, I have to confess)
And found myself exclaiming
Well, glory be, my child, what a lovely dress.

And meant it but suddenly thought can the glory of God
Reside in a beautiful dress on a girl.
Is it not of the Devil's making?
Think of music and think of a dress awhirl.

Last night my cousin came home from sea and we all
Wend down to Matt's for a couple of jars,
And a stranger fiddler was playing
And I walked home late and unsteady under the stars.

So standing alone at the altar this morning, father,
With the body of Christ in my hands I said
The words without thought of their meaning
And last night's new reel ran round and round in my head.

THE PRINT

They have taken the body away
But have left him here.
Day-old tobacco smoke
Meets you at the door
Of the unwarmed house.

Food waits on the table,
A last shopping,
And fumbled lists.
A vest is hanging to dry.
With what ingenuity
The old survive.
Here in stains and dust
Is the print of how it is done.

By water and fire
A weeping detective
Destroys the evidence.

GOODBYE

Had he driven them far away, wife and children,
Without knowing how. Surely they would return?
And now the Radio Times came round so fast,
There were tumbling walls to rebuild and trees to plant,
So much to plan in the house that had been his past.

His litany of defeat you tried to stem
With words and words until time came to go.
How easy that Sunday night to disregard
Why in that bare kitchen, although you promised
To be back within the month, he hugged so hard.

THE QUARRY

The quietness,
They have all scattered
Into the maze of gorse
And slabs of rock,
In tattered jerseys
And faded frocks.

Ages ago,
And I still stand
Caught in the long afternoon
In the old quarry,
Face to the wall,
Counting to twenty.

NEW MOON

The sun is down and the ridge-line
Of trees moves into focus.

Your fields stiffen with frost.
Forget the walk to the hilltop
And the sight of that new moon slipping
Into the sea. Turn home.

Wrapped in their breath
Your cattle stamp at the gate.

INDELICATE

Served by the quiet woman with the brown eyes
In the delicatessen indelicate even to think
That the sound when she turns aside and movingly
Slices salami evokes the jingle of bedsprings.

THREE ITS

It wasn't much,
It wouldn't last long,
A crust and a bottle of water,
And how he was dying to share it.

It was that sort of place,
A kind of Sahara.
If you met someone in the middle of it
You wouldn't call it chance.

The sun lifts into the sky again
To a chorus of bread and water.

PALAIS D'AMOUR

The cabaret comes to climax
At the lit end of a crowded hall
As a mumbling transvestite thrusts
A cup in the air in triumph.

In shadow beside a disturbed
Ocean of heads a watchful madame
In her own space, to her own music,
Dances her baby to sleep.

AS WHEN

As when in a city
Where once you felt at home
You take your place in the café,
And coffee steams, cigar-smoke
Drifts across and voices
Dissolve to liturgy,

As when, faint with walking,
You enter a church,
Sit at the end of a pew
Alone in a great vault
And listen for silence,

As when you slip into a bar
With its glass and mahogany,
Put down your drink,
Settle yourself in a corner
And close your eyes,

Time wavers,
Time falls away.

If a passing angel
Proposed you build an altar
You would no more demur

Than you would to raise a cairn,
Above the forest,
Above the cloud,
In the shiver of dawn on a peak.

A CADENCE

In tremulous script he wished a Happy Christmas
And Bright New Year to the widow of his friend
On the flyleaf of *British Flora*, and there he added:
My mother and I used this when we went for walks
Beyond Queen's Road when I was a little boy
Between 1884 and 89
And in those days we found many wild flowers
In the summer by the banks of the Mersey.

THE SLOW WAY

The slow way home was through the wood
Which creaked with age

And down the steep slope
Which gorse was rewinning

And, as light failed,
Along the green lane where water streamed

And in the November storm
The red campion battled so late.

MORE THAN GLASS

Speeding by train to a city
To a sad cremation,
Cut off by more than glass
From the bloomed hayfields,
From the child with satchel standing
In morning sun at the end of a lane.

PEACE

How come you find peace
In the heart of a city
With three old women
And one young man

In a fusty cavity
Where the hopes of uncounted prayers
And nuptials and requiems
Spiral and hang

Like cigarette smoke
At the height of a party
Eternally.

SILENCE

Dead?

From a window?

Was she depressed?

The receiver reposes.

The drop of silence
Becomes a lake.

FIRST NIGHT

Open-eyed in bed,
Effigies on a tomb,
Outside is starry and bright-rimmed
Clouds are traversing the window
Making their quick condolence.

Deep in a new first night,
Past all but holding hands,
Not a word, not a stir, nor now
Any sobs any more.

HILLFORT

This hazy unwonted
Dry October draught
From the hills to the east
Has blanched the fields,
Has crusted the mud in the gateways.

Has impaled on the gorse
Of the scarry ramparts
A shivering array
Of votive bronze and gold
From the hangings below.

Poised on the rim,
The ancient ones,
The thorn with its haws
And oak with the last
Of its leaves bow into the wind.

THE ORNITHOLOGIST'S FRIEND

The ornithologist, like a doctor
Pronouncing my dissolution, said they were gone.
Lapwings which years ago had abandoned the lowlands
Could no longer be found in the hills, not in these parts.

But he was wrong, for two peewits cry
As they stumble and slide in air like men in snowdrifts
Above the field by the mountain road where I walked
With a headful of sounds which came from no creature on earth.

No, my darlings, I've too many secrets already.
What would I give to know that you had kept yours,
To find you in twelve months' time drunkenly wheeling,
Summoning me away from your airy domain
Where the gelding stands alone in the field full of rushes.

AT THE ROOT OF BEING
From the Welsh of Waldo Williams

At the root of being there is no decay,
The heartwood survives.
Courage there is the tenderness
Of the life of all frail lives.

That is where after the storm the heart withdraws.
The world's not right,
But in this low redoubt the squirrel of happiness
Makes its nest tonight.

MERCY

Ritual, said the Sister of Mercy,
What words can not express.
She was speaking of bereavement.

Mourners stepped off the boat.
A couple sat on a casing,
Unmoving, no longer young.

What dangers had he survived?
What affection could he have deserved
As he gazed out to sea

While she cushioned her head
On the shoulder of his jacket
And fingered his buttons like a baby?

THE EDGE OF A PLAYGROUND

As disenchantment,
A drawing away
From family,
From attentive loved ones,

Steals, you imagine,
Like dawning light
Regardlessly
To the slowly dying,

So disenchantment
Can strike like lightning
In the calm of a day
With nearest long-no-see-ones,

And strike for instance
At the edge of a playground
Crowded with children.
So little is called for.

Simply two strangers
On a neighbouring seat
Half-watching a child,
Simply a shock of red hair,
A face and a laugh.

THE ROCK

Sea campion in the pocket,
Thrift in the cleft of the rock.
Below, garlands of seaweed,
A tract of sand washed clean
And waves retreating.

Beyond the grey, beyond the green, the blue,
And beyond the blue,
The parting we call the horizon.

A WINTER CALENDAR

A garden expectant,
Hedge-shadows black,
Moonlight shining
From dew on the cabbage leaves.

*

The chestnut stark
In the pale meadow,
Her dress a circle
Of gold on the floor at her feet.

*

Stones hoary,
Molehills like rock,
The thistles withdrawn
To their frosty crystalline core.

*

A frozen stream,
Mouthings,
Words trying to form,
Bubbles under the ice.

*

Clouds build,
The moon goes under,
Sleepless companions
Hear the rain arrive.

*

A last tattoo
And the squall is past,
Gutters quaver,
A blackbird begins to sing.

WOODSMOKE

We followed the footpath through the wood.
There was the house,
Its ivy-gripped stone,
Its primrosy garden stepped to a river
Loud in a rock-strung bed.

The gamekeeper we had reckoned on meeting
Was on his rounds.
But his young wife
Had us sit down and we talked of spring
And the shelteredness of the place.

You're the first to have called all winter, she laughed
As we said goodbye.
And my hand lingered
In the hand of the child on the arm of the woman
Of the hose that was drenched in woodsmoke.

AL POCO GIORNO
After Dante

Alas! We have come to the long sweeping shadow
And the short day, to the whitening of the hills
As the summer colour fades from the grass.
And still my tender longing remains green
As ever, though rooted on the cruel stone
Which speaks and hears as though it were a lady.

So alas this extraordinary lady
Stands frigid, as the snow within the shadow;
For she is not moved any more than stone
By the spring sunshine that warms the hills,
Turning them once more from white to green,
Covering them with flowers and with grass.

When she appears, her head wreathed in grass,
Displaced are thoughts of any other lady;
So beautifully formed about the green,
The golden waves lure love into their shadow,
Love who has bound me between the little hills
A thousand times more firmly than cemented stone.

Her beauty is more pure than precious stone;
Her wounds will not be soothed by healing grass;
I have struggled over plains and hills
Trying to escape this fatal lady;
And from her light no wall afforded shadow,
Neither did sheer mountain, nor forest's green.

I have seen her so lovely, dressed in green,
That she would have planted in the hardest stone
The love that I accord her very shadow;

So I have wooed her in a soft field of gras,
Fragrant and tempting as any lady,
And sheltered low among the highest hills.

Indeed, the streams will flow back to the hills
Before this young sapling, fresh and green,
Catch fire from me (as should a loving lady),
From me who would endure to sleep in stone
My whole life, and pasture in fields of grass,
Could I but gaze where glides her mantle's shadow.

Where there falls from the hills the blackest shadow,
Beneath a brilliant green this gracious lady
Drowns it, as one buries a stone in the grass.

III

UNCOLLECTED POEMS

GOLDBERG VARIATIONS

No more today
Than all those years ago
Would I dare approach
The girl in the camelhair coat
Who walked away
After the Sunday recital
In the Corn Exchange
Alone into the damp
Of a fenny November dusk.

So many variations
Vanishing into the mist.

WHEN THE LARK SANG

Someone built and lived in this fallen house
And enclosed a garden on the mountainside,
And others came and harboured happiness
When the lark sang above the lichened stones,
Sang above the close-cropped hummocky ground,
The skeletal thorn trees and the skulls of sheep.

BLOCKS

So cities are built
And lives are built,
Stone on stone.
And block on block,
Red and yellow,
Blue and green,
On the squared carpet
By application
Of your eighteen months'
And my lifetime's experience
Edifices rise.

Till patience snaps
In showers of laughter.
Chastened,
We restore and extend.
Again a hurricane reaps,
Again we build.
But the prophet has spoken:
Of these temples and towers
There will remain
No block on block
By the time we kiss goodnight.

THE LONG GARDEN

Fifty years the long garden
He dug and had watched it yield
All he'd known how to offer
For his bed and board and love.

As on her funeral day
Cloud shadows leapt the hillside.
Where snow had then still lingered
Blackthorn was dressed up in white.

The bag of seed potatoes
He'd stored and how could he ask
The neighbour not to bring dung?
The loam cried to be cherished.

And now the house was empty.
His bent figure bowed again,
His foot pressed down on the spade,
His eye measured the furrow.

THE OLD MAN AND HIS MARE
From the Welsh of Gwynne Williams, published in 1973.
I took to the poem at once.

Despite the fragments of sunshine
It is hard for a man
Feeble-chested
To swing his sickle
Through the graveyard stubble
Before the black clouds
Bring rain to the hay
And dust to the soil

He must hurry
To cut and carry it home
To strengthen the legs
Of the wobbly foal that frisks
In the dewy meadow
Behind the eyelids
Of the home-farm stallion
When he hears the old man and his mare
Slow clip-clopping
Towards the graveyard.

OLD PSYCHIC

A widow,
She lived round the corner,
And since her marriage
London had been her home,
But she was Welsh, and proud of it,
A girl from the valleys.

She called me in
To mend her electric fire,
Then made me tea.
'I can read minds, you know.
Old Psychic, they call me.
I could see you were a good man.

Sid's grateful too.
He's been watching you all along.
Up there.
On the mantlepiece.
In the urn.'

FRAYING CLOUDS

Fraying clouds stream
In a tide-race across the window.
The tops of the sycamore
Sway at their moorings.
The street has fallen quiet;
School has begun.

Nobody and nothing
Are in our midst
Where two are gathered together
In somebody's bed
In nobody's name.

CATATONIC SCHIZOPHRENIA 1995

Why am I here?
It was like a dream.
I've had no life.
Since thirteen I've never
Known where I was.
What can I live for?
Never had a home.
No self-respect.
I can't go out,
Can't face everyone
Staring at me.
God, O God.
It can't go on.
It can't go on, you know.

Two men sit on a bed
In a bare room.
The silences grow longer.
For a moment the courtyard brightens.
The low December sun
Shines on a pinboard,
On its single adornment
Dangling askew,
The Patient's Charter.

HMS *THETIS*

After all but a lifetime gone, I hear it again
So close to home. What I heard in imagination
That evening my uncle called by at my grandparents' home
Having been with the crowd on the beach,
So full of the story.
And Thetis, no more than a name, came into my life.

Again and again.
That tapping from the hull of the sunken submarine.

A KITE'S FLIGHT

She comes like a dream, unbidden,
Usurping a place that was yours,
Repeating endearments, embracing me tight,
She whom we laughingly spoke of;
Insomnia, Queen of the Night.

For hours I can think of you thinking
Only a kite's flight away
But can no longer tell what you choose to remember
Now you observe new vigils,
You too, these nights of November.

Now you sit up in bed and suckle
A child who disrupts your sleep
With demands more unabashed than ever
Were whispered through fingertips
In the watches of night by your lover.

THE LIFELINE

It ought to be simple to tell the truth,
To let some trust
Once more begin to grow,
To tell her the seven-year dalliance is over,
That you fell out of love with me
Quite a while ago,
Yes, quite a while ago.

It ought to be simple to bring her peace,
To end the deceit
And in a few words sever
The lifeline to you that my hands can no longer release,
And tell her you love me no more.
But no, I could never,
Not for my life, I could never.

And while I may sometimes seek you out
And we sit and talk,
How it would ease her pain
To know you can hardly wait for me to go.
Love, when it withers (my darling,
As though you did not know),
Never springs again,
Never springs the same again.

HONEY

Unable to forget,
Beginning another day,
Watching the window,
Letting her coffee stand,
Hearing the magpies chatter,
Watching the treetops sway.

Watching the cobwebs quiver
Between the shooting brambles
And spikes of agrimony,
Holding back her tears,
Spinning her spoonful of honey.

IN NORTH JAPAN

Half an hour away
The Shinkansen races.
We have turned towards the mountains,

Turned up the wooded valley
With its necklace of tiny fields.
'You must see our shrine', says our host.

She pulls off the road, we walk
To a shelf beneath a sun-warmed
Cliff above the river,

Walk through the vermillion gateway
Past clipped azaleas,
Past stone lanterns.

There, backed into a cave
(Where arrowheads were found),
The shrine, perched on stilts,

And within it, seated in darkness,
The giant roughly carved
Glowering wooden god

Placated perhaps for today
By a row of fresh offerings
Of fruit and flowers.

THREE SISTERS

One could not rest
Until she'd bestowed
Her treasure of love.

One could not rest
Until she'd conferred
Her bounty of secrets.

And one could not rest
Until she'd exhausted
Her largesse of guilt.

DEW

Golden sky,
The last people
In twos and ones
In the park as the dew falls.

THE BURIAL

So we come to our primitive masterpiece, 'The Burial',
One of the few of its genre to come out of Wales.
The scene is set by the box-like church in the background,
By the humped sheep-dotted hills and the looming mountain.
The design derives its strength from the dark zig-zag
Of straggling mourners waiting to file past the grave.
Notice the way the untrained hand has captured
The silvery strip of sky between mountain and cloud,
The dramatic splash of white of the minister's surplice,
The shine on the wet gravestones and the wet grass.
But what of the magpie sat on the roof of the church?
And what of the mourner with her red umbrella?
The painting like all true art has its mysteries.
Scholars have even wondered whether the man
In cap and shabby jacket standing hunched
Between the yew trees, gazing out of the picture,
Who might be the gravedigger might not indeed be the artist.

EIGHT YEARS ON

Over the top at dawn?
Yes, on a summer's morning.
We were told it was going to be easy.
We'd just walk over.
They mowed us down like grass.

The shrapnel caught him.
I stopped though I knew he'd had it.
I tried to push his brains back into his head.
Imagine your pal like that.
What else could I do?

What else could I do?
It wasn't a time to act normal.
Did I cry? Did I shed tears?
Probably, probably,
And many, many times since.

LAY-BY

Three hours from the city,
Taking a breath of the mountains,
My elbows rest on a wall

And inches away
A multitude
Shyly returns my gaze:

Tufted hair grass,
Nameless bents and sedges,
Hawkweed, sorrel in bloom,

Bending towards me,
Whispering
We thought you would never come.

SALT

He fretted after his wife died and no one could fathom
His restlessness, it seemed so much more than grieving
To his children who questioned and wondered and looked for signs.
Until the day he stood up: 'I have to tell you.
I just can't go to that place where you've buried your mother,
Ringed by trees and the rock face. I cannot go there.
I have to smell the sea and watch the sunsets.
You know where they buried my shipmates' –
That treeless close-cropped graveyard atilt to the cliff-edge –
'It's there I must go'. He looked at them each in turn.
And the children stared back at the now serene-looking father
Who no more believed in God than a resurrection.

COMFORT

By the ear, not the eye,
Comfort creeps in.
An angel-whisper,
A word, a talisman
From a weathered song,
Or music, wordless.

Yet through the eye
An afternoon
Of lowering cloud,
Of turbulent greys,
The landscape already
Dissolved to dusk,
Can startle you
With equal comfort.

A distant field,
So green, so lit
For a long minute
By an unseen sun.
And slowly occluded,
The greenness leaps
From hill to hill
Like a hand in blessing.

LOST COVE
After visiting Lucas Myers in Tennessee

For half a lifetime he had described to friends
The remote wood with its lake where he would build –
After a vagrant life, in a place that would echo
The lost cove of his childhood – a final home.

And here we had come on a visit, walking in file
Beneath the high canopy, stooping below
Half fallen trunks, bending saplings aside,
Descending a track that years ago had been cleared
When he bought the wood with a small inheritance.

We dropped to the edge of the lake.
Footprints of deer patterned the muddy verge.
Young tulip poplars soared into the sky
Where turkey buzzards circled. Gravely discussing
Where best the house could stand, we stood and pondered.

Below the lake, along the half-buried stream,
He led us down to the glade. Here, he said,
Under the laurel trees he used to sit.
We too now sat on mossy stones. We watched
A water snake slide in the sluggish water.

A silence fell. The grossness of our presence
Beside the gossamer delicacy of the vision
Of the youthful dream we paid our homage to
Disturbed our minds. How utterly far removed
Was the envoi that with a flourish of the hand
Had served to dismiss a thousand defeats and rebuffs,
His 'What the hell. Let's have a drink', a gesture
Whose very shadow would now have profaned the moment,
To be ushered away like the drunk at a funeral.

A HEART

How can I reproach
A heart long past
Three score and ten
That with all its might
Thumps so unsteadily
Hour after hour
In the caverns of night.

How can I blame you –
You who took flight
From my vortex of folly
And kept your distance –
If I find you haunting
That cavernous space.

Or blame a heart
Here in daylight
When I look down a street
And glimpse a figure
That could for a moment
Almost be yours.

DEBRIS

Like a pyromaniac
With a match in his hand
And a can of petrol,

Like an errant lover
Recalling a long-held gaze,
Hand on the phone,

Like a lone castaway
Sealing his cry in a bottle
To be thrown to the waves,

A bright-eyed God
Conjures from nothingness
Plus and minus,

And crossing himself,
Begins his countdown,
Steeled for the bang.

He can no more calculate
Where the debris will fly
Than know who is going to love him.

THE TRUTH

Let the painful truth come home.
You've had your stay and uttered
In stumbling words what little
You ever had need to tell.
She listened and marked your words,
Forgoing any comment.

Unlike a wife or lover
Or a friend, dining *á deux*,
She will not take it amiss
And graciously may even
Bestow a tacit blessing
And consent to meet your eye

If you sit out the meal in silence.

GORSE

How ever you arrived here
To huddle against this slab,
Perhaps as a homing bird,
Perhaps a storm-blown vagrant,
Here where the lichened shoulders
Of rock erupt through the turf,
Where the evening sky deepens
And a wind chill off the sea
Blows constant, unimpeded
By the tumble-down stone walls,
You have come on failing legs,
Lain down, curled up, found comfort,
To sleep the sleep of ages
In the numb embrace of cold.

And awake, purged and shriven,
At one with granules of soil
Nourishing this gnarled thicket
Of gorse with its hundred points
Of gold that no more than love
Are ever out of season.

A SURVIVOR

His last companions swallowed up in the desert
And he, holed up by day, trekking by twilight,
Spectral, early one morning, enters the town,
Down a street of women in veils, of beasts and beggars,
Of furtive huddles of men
Eyeing him distantly.

All is on edge. After the heat of noon
When people re-emerge,
In a shady corner of the square
He waits, sick with foreboding,
And prays that confronting the taunting crowd
There will be beside him
A quiet man to stoop
And write in the dust with his finger.

THE HOB

In an absence of mind, watching the porridge bubble,
My eye is caught by the shine from the black hob
Of a tranquil pool of palest amethyst
Deep below.

A pool crossed all of a sudden
By a darting minnow,
A creature bewitched
Only moments later
Into a far-away kite
Riding the morning sky.

THE PEBBLE

How could you not keep it for ever?
This non-descript pebble,
This fleck of creation,
Handed to you in passing
At the water's edge
On a crowded beach
Mutely
By a small boy
With a look of recognition.

It stirs
And it moves the stars.

UMBRELLAS

Declining the proffered lift, they decided to walk.
The path was unlit and puddled, the common squelchy.
And after ten minutes they had to turn back. Whose fault was it? His.
Oh, his. She piled on the blame till he shouted and furiously
Flung the two folded umbrellas into the hedge
And shocked himself into his senses and squatted and groped
Among the hedge-roots and litter to find them, and meanwhile
She had walked off and, when he then followed, she'd gone,
Was nowhere in sight, perhaps she'd raced on or had wondered
Away to the river, so he returned to the circle
Of light from a lamp by the gate where they'd entered and there
Came this moon-faced hulk of a man walking his dogs
In the dark and the drizzle demanding to know of the stranger
What he was doing. 'Looking for your wife?', an incredulous
Look, 'Oh yeah, and don't you talk posh' and guffawed
As the dogs ran up and started to bark at this creature
In search of a wife by the gate of the common and laughed
Again and called to his barking dogs 'Let him be,
He's cultured. Don't be so working class'. And grinned
As the dogs continued to bark and the rain came down
On the man and his dogs and the husband and lamp and trees
And an angry umbrella-less wife somewhere out in the darkness.

THE BED

She, with mother and aunt
And two prams
And five more children,
Snaked across Germany
Fleeing the Russians,
Sleeping in barns and in ruins,
Bargaining, foraging,
Towards the West.
And now, in a majestic
Mechanised bed,
She enters the day
With a cornucopia
Of riddles and echoes,
'Where am I?', 'Are you my husband?'
'You must hoover the children's room
And make a bed for my mother.'

IV

OCCASIONAL POEMS

BIRTHDAY POEM FOR JEAN HAWKES

Jean Hawkes, translator, died soon after celebrating her 90th birthday.

In the far-away '70s when youth went long-haired
And girls dressed like gipsies and life held no fears,
I recall two good mothers, Edrica and Jean,
Who would pick up the fallen and wipe away tears.

And David meanwhile would get on with his books
And dig his allotment, and charm us all.
But he felt the oppression of Dreaming Spires
And dons and meetings and dinners in hall.

He'd spent so many years with his ancient poets
Alone on their mountains in mist and gales.
Solitude beckoned and David was drawn
To find his retreat in innermost Wales.

A stout little house on a stony hill
Where foxes and buzzards and kites would appear,
A lime-hungry garden for David to dig,
A welcoming hearth where Jean kept good cheer.

But family and comfort then made a late call.
The highland adventure now drew to a close.
It was farewell to Wales and a gentle return
To the meadows of Iffley and well-earned repose.

Remembering sorrows, remembering joys,
In Minehead your family gathers again
For a birthday, dear Jean: long cherish the day
With serenity born of your four score and ten.

TO TED HUGHES ON HIS APPOINTMENT AS POET LAUREATE

(*To the tune of* The Night Before Larry was Stretched)

For months the Queen was perplexed
The Palace fell into a tizzy
The Ladies in waiting were vexed
The equerries were nervously busy
In the broad shires of England the sound
Of panic trilled in the boscage.
A Laureate had to be found.
A Queen cannot rule without language
Or nourish her people on pap.

With the court in the coils of despair
And bewilderment gripping the country
A voice came from God knows where
(Or was it an owl in an Oaktree?)
Ted Hughes, did you say, who is he?
He is no-one who I had my shirt on
A bard who's fought long in the sea?
A farmer from slow deep Devon
With an eye for the eye of a muse?

So her majesty made her choice
She wills that this truth should be written
That a sansculotte be the voice
Of the hidden domains of Britain
For Ted was always your man
When any poor word was in trouble:
As a glittering talisman
It will shyly emerge from the rubble
To sit with its pals in a row.

He will suffer the great and the wise,
The bore, the critic, the grafter,
Knowing an antidote lies
In an evening of crack and laughter.
And when in the fire's fading light
The company starts to be drowsy
He will slide off into the night
With the one he loves better than any
Whom he still owes a word or two.

LETTER TO TED AND LUKE

During the 1960s, Lucas Myers, a very close friend of Ted Hughes and mine, lived in Paris. He would make short visits to Ted, at Court Green, and to me in Wales. On some evenings during these visits Luke would engage us in the game of writing a joint poem, each poet taking alternate lines. The poem below is my reply to one such joint poem sent from Court Green. Carol Hughes found it after Ted's death and returned it to me.

What do two old bums on the rump of the world have to worry about?
If they've got a tick about something at least they needn't shout.
Who cares if it's a drop of beer or of blood you've got on your snout.

Is their aim to expel their inflated ennui in the bray of their trumpet?
You'd think they'd drunk London dry or gobbled the last bit of crumpet
And even in that case I think they could sit themselves down and lump it.

Here I'd chewed through a bitch of a day and spat out the last piece of gristle
And got home to my missus for a nice cup of cha to wet my whistle
When what should she hand me to read but a scurrilous epistle

From the bums aforesaid who bloody well ought to have had more tact
Than to pelt a man with words when he's come home just about whacked
And it isn't as if their hippety-hop lines were certified fact.

Indeed I thought their pretention might possibly be poetic
And I consulted the English Professor but he looked at me somewhat pathetic
So I tried my psychiatrist friend 'It's a pretty fearsome emetic

Your acquaintances must have got on to' he told me right out straight
And frankly there are features of their malady it were better to isolate
And they'd better run off for attention double-quick before it's too late.

Meanwhile to be going on with I'll pass on a little advice
Concerning Contact with Women: though by all accounts it is nice
To use eyes and fingers and whatnot its safer to use mice

At least first to see how they fare as sort of guinea-pigs
And if they return alive still behave like the prince of prigs
For casual hetero chit-chat can apparently lead to jig-a-jigs,

A sort of chronic condition against which doctors warn
Which can make a man feel ungrateful for the blessing of having been born,
Make him feel like a speck of mud on the tip of a Rhinoceros horn.

And lastly one word about drink: when you think you spy palmy lands
And the concubines beckon it soon will have you laid low in the sands
With your guts in despair, your toes in the air and your head in your hands.

        And Sloth said 'Basta!'
        And I said 'Master!'